To: S

Love, Nana
Baba

W9-CMH-361

# Trains
## on the Go

by Anne J. Spaight

BUMBA BOOKS™

LERNER PUBLICATIONS • MINNEAPOLIS

**Note to Educators:**

Throughout this book, you'll find critical thinking questions. These can be used to engage young readers in thinking critically about the topic and in using the text and photos to do so.

Copyright © 2017 by Lerner Publishing Group, Inc.

All rights reserved. International copyright secured. No part of this book may be reproduced, stored in a retrieval system, or transmitted in any form or by any means—electronic, mechanical, photocopying, recording, or otherwise—without the prior written permission of Lerner Publishing Group, Inc., except for the inclusion of a brief quotation in an acknowledged review.

Lerner Publications Company
A division of Lerner Publishing Group, Inc.
241 First Avenue North
Minneapolis, MN 55401 USA

For reading levels and more information, look up this title at www.lernerbooks.com.

**Library of Congress Cataloging-in-Publication Data**

The Cataloging-in-Publication Data for *Trains on the Go* is on file at the Library of Congress.
ISBN 978-1-5124-1447-9 (lib. bdg.)
ISBN 978-1-5124-1485-1 (pbk.)
ISBN 978-1-5124-1486-8 (EB pdf)

Manufactured in the United States of America
1 – VP – 7/15/16

LERNER
SOURCE

Expand learning beyond the printed book. Download free, complementary educational resources for this book from our website, www.lernerresource.com.

# Table of
# Contents

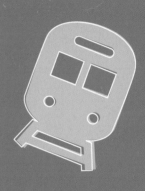

# Moving Trains

Trains run on tracks.

They carry people and things.

Trains are made of cars.

These cars are joined together.

Some trains have many cars.

Some have few.

People ride in some cars.

These cars are comfortable.

Some cars have snacks and drinks.

**Why might people choose to ride trains?**

Other cars carry cargo.

Some cars hold liquids.

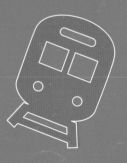

The engine is the first car.

It powers the train.

Long trains have two or more engines.

**Why would long trains need more engines?**

13

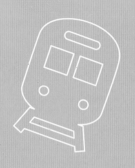

The engineer works in the

engine car.

He controls the train.

He stops the train with its

brakes.

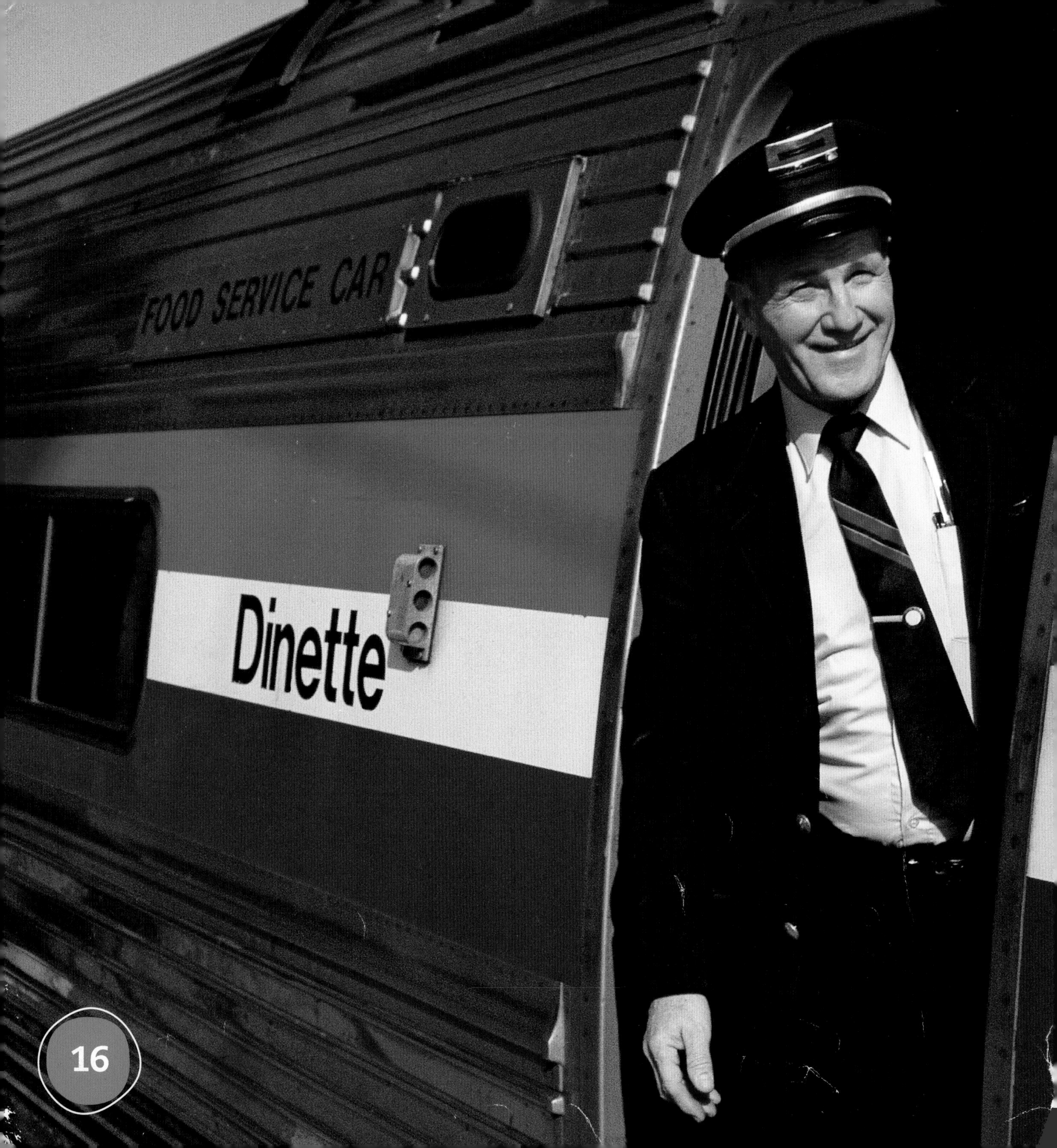
FOOD SERVICE CAR
Dinette

The conductor helps the train's crew work together.

He also helps people enjoy their trip.

Signals are near the track.

They tell the engineer to slow down.

Other signals tell people a train is coming.

**Why do you think signals are important?**

Trains are important.

They bring supplies across the country.

They take people places too.

Riding the train is fun!

# Parts of a Train

car

engine

track

wheels

22

# Picture Glossary

**cargo**

the things a train carries

**conductor**

the person who helps the train's crew work together

**engineer**

the person who makes the train stop and go

**tracks**

a pair of metal bars that trains move on

23

# Index

# Read More

Hill, Lee Sullivan. *Trains on the Move.* Minneapolis: Lerner Publications, 2011.

Rogers, Hal. *Trains.* Mankato, MN: The Child's World, 2014.

Silverman, Buffy. *How Do Trains Work?* Minneapolis: Lerner Publications, 2016.

## Photo Credits

The images in this book are used with the permission of: © i4lcocl2/Shutterstock.com, pp. 5, 23 (bottom right); © Jia Li/Shutterstock.com, pp. 6–7; © Pavel L Photo and Video/Shutterstock.com, p. 8; © George Spade/Shutterstock.com, pp. 10–11, 23 (top left); © Albert Pego/Shutterstock.com, p. 13; © auremar/Shutterstock.com, pp. 14–15, 23 (bottom left); © Joseph Sohm/Shutterstock.com, pp. 16, 23(top right); © genyuan huang/iStock.com, p. 19; © Supannee Hickman/Shutterstock.com, p. 20; © Kenneth Sponsler/Shutterstock.com, p. 22.

Front Cover: © Albert Pego/Shutterstock.com.